Original title:
Desert Bloom Dreams

Copyright © 2025 Creative Arts Management OÜ
All rights reserved.

Author: Juliette Kensington
ISBN HARDBACK: 978-1-80566-703-2
ISBN PAPERBACK: 978-1-80566-988-3

The Phoenix of Flora among Winds

In a land where cacti wear hats,
A sneaky lizard whispers to rats.
The blooms have kicklines in the heat,
Like disco dancers, they can't be beat.

With petals popping like confetti,
They laugh at the sun, feeling ready.
A butterfly sneezes, oh what a sight,
While the sun takes a nap, a sleepy delight.

Blossoms in the Embrace of the Desert

Petals giggle under the sun,
Each bloom declares, 'We are number one!'
Cacti tell tales of dramatic intrigue,
While succulents dance with a funky league.

The sands throw a party, no need for a cue,
Blossoms wear sandals, oh if they only knew.
Butterflies host a wild tea party spree,
While sand dunes cheer, 'Be what you want to be!'

Tracing Footprints through Petal Dreams

With every step, the flowers giggle,
A cactus tries hard not to wiggle.
Footprints lead to laughter and games,
As petals whisper the silliest names.

Bees buzz in rhythm, a perfect beat,
While lizards break dance, oh what a feat!
They trace the sun, then hide in the shade,
In a world where even shadows get played.

The Eternal Dance of Sand and Sprout

In the whirl of sandy pirouettes,
Cacti don boots, making new bets.
Petals whirl, twirling like crazy,
Each ounce of wind feels a bit hazy.

Dancing twisters in a flowered parade,
The sun sings loudly, it can't be delayed.
With each gust, giggles erupt in the air,
Even the moon can't help but stare.

Nuances of Parched Earth

In the sand, a cactus grins,
With a hat made of twigs it wins.
A worm pulls a dance, so spry,
While the sun just rolls on by.

A tumbleweed wears shades of blue,
Sipping sunlight like it's brew.
The lizard struts in style so grand,
Holding court on the hot, dry land.

Harmony in Hues

There's a flower that sings a tune,
Beneath the light of a frowning moon.
Its petals dance, though it's quite rare,
With wishes tossed in the airy glare.

A chameleon plays peek-a-boo,
Changing colors while sipping dew.
He calls the ants to join the fun,
As they march 'round like they've won a run.

The Spirit of Survival

A snake wears a bow tie of brown,
As he slithers through this dry town.
He tells jokes to the passing ants,
While dreaming of fancy pants.

The sunburnt rock starts to hum,
Cracks a smile, then starts to drum.
The critters gather for a show,
While tumbleweeds begin to flow.

Floral Mirage

A mirage of petals floats on by,
Painting wishes in the sky.
A prankster bee begins to tease,
While sipping nectar from a breeze.

The flowers giggle in a row,
As butterflies put on a show.
With every twist and every twirl,
They turn this place into a whirl.

Surreal Cacti Symphony

In a land where shadows play,
Cacti dance like they're in a ballet.
With arms that reach for the sun,
They giggle and twirl, just having fun.

A cactus in a top hat, oh so dapper,
Twirling around like a clumsy capper.
Nature's pun, the spines make them wise,
But watch out, they see through your disguise!

Sun-Kissed Reverie

Under the sun, the cacti grin,
Joking in the heat, as they begin.
With sunhats perched on their prickly heads,
They sip lemonade, ignoring their beds.

Lizards join in the sunny affair,
Playing cards in the warm desert air.
Each laugh echoes, a mirthful cheer,
In this wild haven, we gather near.

Drought's Daring Canvas

In a dry world, colors burst alive,
Painted with laughter, we all thrive.
Each flower's a joker, bright and bold,
Telling secrets that never get old.

A cactus in shades of neon lie,
Winks at the clouds, daring them to cry.
With a pop and a sizzle, rain might play,
But the sun's too busy, it's here to stay!

Thorns and Blossoms

With thorns so sharp, and blossoms so sweet,
They argue at night, in a prickly heat.
"Your colors are loud!" the thorns always chide,
"Yet without me, dear flower, you cannot abide!"

Together they laugh, a hilarious pair,
Sharing their woes on a sun-kissed chair.
In their quirky brawl, life's truth is found,
Even prickly opposites can be profound!

Blooms that Dance in the Grit

In the sandy stretch where the sun does shine,
Tiny flowers twirl, as if on a line.
They wear their lives like a quirky hat,
Shaking their petals, going 'How about that?'

Cacti giggle, holding their prickly stance,
While wind-blown seeds join in the dance.
Sure, they're stuck in this parched old land,
But they groove and sway, oh isn't it grand?

The Lament of the Withering Flower

A flower sat sulking, feeling quite blue,
 'Why can't I wear a colorful shoe?
All of my friends have umbrellas of cheer,
 While here I stand, looking wan and sheer.'

A bee buzzed near, with a wink and a grin,
 'Though you're a bit wilted, you still can win!
Just shake off the dirt and let laughter abound,
 Your petals can shine in this dry, gritty ground.'

Oasis Whispers of Hope and Rebirth

In a pocket of sand where the waters flow,
A mirage appears, putting on a show.
Dancers of color spring from the well,
Singing sweet songs — oh, can you hear them yell?

They flutter and flounce in a joyous parade,
Bobbing their heads, all memories fade.
'It's never too late for a little surprise,
Just look to the sky and dream super-sized!'

Where Sunlight Kisses the Thorns

A rose made a fuss, feeling prickly and cross,
'Why does everyone think that I'm such a loss?
Thorns are just part of my glamorous style,
Really, I'm just like the rest — in denial!'

The sunbeams chuckled, warming her mood,
'Embrace your sharp edges, don't be so crude!
With laughter and light, you'll astonish the day,
Even the thorns get to laugh in their way!'

Scenting the Air with Sunlit Love

Cacti wear their spines with grace,
As bumblebees dance, a frantic race.
The sun's a bright and cheeky chap,
Who plays hide and seek in a yellow cap.

Sand dunes giggle, shifting their forms,
While tumbleweeds plot in playful swarms.
A felt hat perched on a lizard's head,
Sips on sunshine, and dreams of bread.

The Mirage of Everlasting Color

Oh, how the flowers tease and twirl,
In a swirling dance, they laugh and whirl.
Hot winds whisper silly, joyful tunes,
While lizards bask under playful moons.

A roadrunner in sneakers races by,
With a cheeky wink and a sprightly sigh.
Petals burst in colors so bold,
Making rainbows blush, their tales unfold.

Resilience in Every Petal's Glow

In cracked earth, the blooms play hide and seek,
While the sun's embrace makes them laugh and squeak.
Little drips of rain, a comical spree,
Creating puddles where dance parties be!

Sassy succulents, wearing bright hats,
Invite the sun to join in their chats.
With roots so deep, they wiggle and sway,
In this land of oddities, they love to play.

Sun-Kissed Secrets of the Barren

In the vastness, secrets flicker and twine,
Colorful whispers in the warmth divine.
A chubby rabbit steals the sun's bright rays,
Raising giggles in the golden haze.

When the sun sets in a sultry grin,
The flowers chuckle, let the laughter spin.
Even in silence, the night can glow,
With fireflies giggling, putting on a show.

The Arid Dreamers' Reverie

In a land where cacti dance,
The sand calls out for a chance.
Lizards in suits look quite grand,
Holding a meeting on shifting sand.

A rabbit in shades sips cold tea,
Laughing at clouds that never agree.
While tumbleweeds tell each tall tale,
Of the great rains that always fail.

Beneath the Heat

Under the sun that seems to melt,
A cactus wears a hat it felt.
Chasing shadows, they play tag,
While saguaro dreams of a green brag.

A mirage of tacos flows by,
With a side of chips that can't fly.
Sipping mirth from a cactus' spout,
While the sun just laughs and shouts.

Life Awakens

When the sun blinks and starts to tease,
The flowers giggle and share their cheese.
Cacti claim they're the funniest bunch,
While dandelions throw a lunchtime brunch.

The breeze knows all the secret jokes,
It tickles the feet of the wandering folks.
They trip on laughter, or so it seems,
In a world that spins with silly dreams.

A Tapestry Woven with Dust and Light

Threads of laughter in every hue,
Stitched with shadows, a clever crew.
A sunbeam breaks into a dance,
While the dust bunnies take their chance.

Breezes hum a silly tune,
As the moon joins in for a cartoon.
Colors twirl and whirl in delight,
Painting the whispers of day and night.

When Mirage Meets Reality

When wishful sights throw a soft prank,
A lake of laughter fills the bank.
Cacti blink with mischievous glee,
As they hold hands with a passing bee.

The horizon grins with a sly wink,
Promising drinks that never sink.
In this land of dreamy schemes,
Reality chuckles, bursting the seams.

Oasis of Forgotten Fragrance

In the sand, a stench so sly,
A cactus wears a flower tie.
I think it's trying to impress,
But bees just laugh, then make a mess.

A mirage gives a wink today,
It looks like an all-you-can-slay.
But all I find is a lizard's sigh,
Wishing for wings, oh my, oh my!

Cactus Serenade Under the Stars

At night the prickly guys do sing,
To the tune of a tumbleweed fling.
"Don't poke me," one cactus said,
"Unless you want a thorny bed!"

The moonlight sparkles like spilled cream,
While owls are lost in a cactus dream.
They'd dance, but feet are quite a mess,
In their barbed shoes they just digress.

Waking in a Sun-Baked Garden

Awake to find my hat is fried,
The sun has turned my coffee dried.
Plants water themselves with a wink,
While I just sit here—oh, how I stink!

A gopher rolls by with a grin,
He offers me a bottle—gin?
"Just kidding!" he chuckles, what a pup,
Instead it's sweat! Cheers! Bottoms up!

Shimmering Hues of Parched Earth

The ground does crack in artistic ways,
A canvas for lizards—a visual maze.
They strut like models on a runway,
Though really, they just hope to play.

Colors shift with the sun's hot glare,
While I sit dreaming of a chair.
"Look at us," they proudly boast,
As I fall asleep—not a moment to toast!

Petal's Journey Through Grit

In the sand where cacti grin,
A petal danced with cheeky spin.
It tripped on rocks, then laughed aloud,
Declared itself the star, so proud.

With every gust that blew its way,
It rolled and tumbled, come what may.
It met a worm, who wore a hat,
And proudly said, "I'm richer than that!"

The sun was hot, the laughter bright,
Our petal twirled, a colorful sight.
In prickly pals and sandy schemes,
It found its way through silly dreams.

At dusk it flopped, so tired and worn,
Yet chuckled at how it had been born.
With grit and glow, it made its case,
Who knew the desert held such grace?

Nature's Quiet Triumph

A little sprout in ankle-high sand,
Said, "Here I am, isn't it grand?"
With cheeky roots that stretched and twirled,
It shook its leaves at the dry, brown world.

The lizards laughed, "You'll never survive!"
But the sprout just nudged its head and thrived.
It bloomed a flower, all yellow and bright,
Declared it'd win the flower fight!

The rain clouds passed but never stopped,
Yet that sprout stood tall, refused to flop.
"Rain's overrated! Just see my show!"
It whispered to a passing crow.

And when at last the rain did fall,
The sprout danced wildly, just like a ball.
"Look at me, I'm nature's prank!"
In triumph now, it proudly drank!

Sands of Whispering Petals

In shifting sands, a whisper flew,
A tiny voice said, "Join my crew!"
Petals piled up in a swirly heap,
With dreams of fun, they wouldn't sleep.

A flat rock yawned, gave a loud cheer,
"Come join the party! The fun is here!"
Dancing petals in a silly line,
With every sway, they felt divine.

An ant popped up with a tiny tune,
Said, "I'll be DJ under the moon!"
The petals laughed, twirled round and round,
In the sands, joy was truly found.

As night wore on, stars came to see,
The party grew as sweet as could be.
With a wink, a rock chimed back a beat,
And petals danced till they fell asleep.

Mirage of a Thousand Blossoms

In a heatwave, colors sparkled bright,
Mirages appeared in pure daylight.
A thousand blossoms, or so it seemed,
Tickled the eye, the mind just dreamed.

They danced in circles, a curious sight,
Chasing shadows, in sheer delight.
"Catch me if you can," a lilac sang,
But then a tumbleweed just went clang!

A cactus poked in with a sly grin,
"Who needs water? I'm fashionably thin!"
The flowers giggled, swayed to the beat,
In their sun-fueled, joyous heat.

As dusk approached, the blooms took flight,
Lifted by giggles, whispers of night.
"A mirage of flowers, a trick of the light,
But laughter's the real, eternal delight!"

Secrets Beneath the Surface

Cacti wear their spines with flair,
As they throw a fancy fair.
Sandy shadows dance at dusk,
Chasing critters, oh so brisk.

Whispers float on hot, dry air,
Napping jackrabbits without a care.
Dunes hold secrets, none shall know,
Except for lizards, stealing the show.

Hush now, hear the tumbleweed,
Its dance moves make the cactus plead.
A mischievous wind starts to tease,
As it shows off with reckless ease.

Underneath this golden sky,
Squirrels gossip as they pass by.
In this land where mirages play,
Funny things happen every day.

Skylines of Succulents

Looming giants in the sun,
Succulents boast, their job's just fun.
Layers of green, so proud and tall,
They chuckle softly at their sprawl.

With eyes full of mischief, they stand,
Mimicking clouds that never land.
Their oversized hats give them grace,
The succulents giggle, keeping pace.

Oh, how they thrive with little care,
While humans fret, and pull their hair.
These wise green beings laugh with glee,
At our cluelessness about their spree.

Growing tall in the blazing heat,
With sidewalk dances that can't be beat.
They poke fun at the passing birds,
Enjoying life without the words.

Timeless Arid Beauty

In this land, where time stands still,
Cacti get taller at their will.
They throw a party; who could resist?
With a prickly dance that can't be missed.

Tumbleweeds roll with comic flair,
Challenge the wind, let's see who dares.
A sagebrush sage, with wisdom deep,
Will nod along, then take a leap.

Even stones share jokes of old,
As laughter mingles with the gold.
Beneath the sun's warm, knowing glance,
Every creature joins in the dance.

As shadows stretch like playful cats,
The desert ball creates awkward chats.
Rattlers tune their rhymes on beat,
While cacti sway to shuffle their feet.

Blossoms in the Heat

Petals open, smiles all around,
In the heat, joy knows no bound.
Dancing flowers in colors bright,
Quip with bees; oh, what a sight!

Sunflowers wave with a cheeky glance,
Inviting the bumblebees to dance.
Though sweat drips and lips do pout,
These blossoms know what life's about.

Bees giggle as they sip their tea,
In this sunny paradise, oh so free.
Even the sun joins in the fun,
Mischief sparkles; let the laughter run!

With lizards donning hats of shade,
They're the star of this bright charade.
In the warmth, we'll hush and swoon,
Kudos to flowers who sing their tune!

The Resilient Heart of Aridity

In a land where cacti do tap dance,
A lizard wears a hat, what a chance!
The sun tickles the ground, oh so hot,
While a tumbleweed rolls in with a splot.

A mirage shows a pool of soda pop,
I sip from it, and my taste buds flop.
The lizards chuckle, and I join in,
Who knew such fun could come from a spin?

Cacti sing tunes about rain that won't,
While roadrunners race with flair that can't.
A jackrabbit dreams of a cooler night,
So, he hops while the stars shine bright.

In this arid land, laughter's our fuel,
Each day is silly, not just a duel.
With each sunbeam that dares peek through,
We find joy, oh yes, in all that we do.

Surreal Gardens of Solitude

In lonely plots where shadows play,
A banana plant dreams of ballet.
Cacti wave their spiny arms wide,
Whispering secrets of the sun's pride.

A tumbleweed spins like a top,
While tumbleweeds frolic and flop.
The willow tree tries to tell jokes,
But windswept leaves just giggle, folks.

Sand dunes debate what shape they should take,
As ants dressed in tuxes get ready to bake.
Meanwhile, a cactus writes poetry all night,
About strange shapes he saw in moonlight.

Each petal that falls brings a laugh anew,
In gardens of solitude where blooms are few.
So, come take a stroll through this whimsical zone,
And enjoy the jest of the sands all alone.

Enchanted Sandscapes Morning Glories

In the morning light, the sands giggle,
As a flower blooms and starts to wiggle.
Mice have parties, they dance in a line,
Where tall sunflowers sip cactus wine.

The sand dunes wear hats, quite absurd,
As bees tell stories that're always blurred.
Each petal from blooms catches the breeze,
Tickling the toes of the buzzing bees.

A prickle bush whispers tales of the moon,
As a squirrel in shades plays a merry tune.
Sun-kissed cacti wear the latest trends,
Making sure each pun doesn't offend.

In a world so dry, joy blossoms bright,
Even the stars join the silly flight.
With laughter echoing for all to hear,
The playful sands bring us laughter and cheer.

Windswept Petals on the Horizon

Windswept petals sail through the air,
Making a ruckus without a care.
An eager cactus hitches a ride,
On a breeze that's swift, and full of pride.

The horizons speak of joyful surprises,
Like tumbleweeds dressed in full disguises.
Dancing with flowers that twirl and spin,
It's a festival that nobody can win!

Each grain of sand has a tale to tell,
Of mirth and laughter and times they fell.
As midday sun springs a playful glow,
The desert ensemble puts on a show.

So let the petals flutter and play,
In the windswept joys of a sunlit day.
Here, even shadows have fun it seems,
In the realm where we chase after dreams.

Echoes of Silent Growth

In the sandy land where cacti play,
A succulent whispers, 'I'm not dead today!'
With arms wide open, they reach for the sun,
They rave in the heat, having such silly fun.

A tumbleweed waltzes, it rolls with a grin,
While lizards just giggle and join in the spin.
The shadows are chuckling, what a sight to see,
As lonesome old rocks claim their victory spree.

Petals wide awake, with colors so bright,
They throw a party under the moonlight.
Butterflies foxtrot, while bees shake a leg,
Nature's own creatures, each dance a new peg.

So let's raise a toast to the prickly and bold,
For laughter and joy, not just stories of old.
Amidst sandy whispers, the joys we can find,
In this wild, quirky world, just let loose your mind.

Sunshine's Hidden Garden

There's a patch of odd veggies, a sight to behold,
Tomatoes in sunglasses, looking so bold.
A carrot's doing yoga, leaves in a twist,
While onions are laughing, 'We're hard to resist!'

Sunflowers gossip, with heads held up high,
They chat about clouds that drift slowly by.
With their funny hats on, they just can't be beat,
In this vibrant garden, life's a quirky treat.

Radishes rally for a tiny parade,
While peas pop and giggle, happily displayed.
All in the sun, they eat lemonade,
As plucky green beans try to serenade.

Don't miss out the bugs, with their wild little jive,
Beetles and crickets, so happy and five!
In this dizzying patch, life's always a game,
In sunshine's embrace, we'll never be the same.

Fluttering Fragrance

A butterfly sneezed, oh what a surprise,
It tickled the roses and brought forth their sighs.
The daisies are dancing, their petals aglow,
While poppies are laughing at grasshoppers' show.

The lavender giggles, scent wafting around,
With bees in a frenzy, they never slow down.
Hummingbirds chuckle as they zoom in and out,
While tulips just stand there, raising a pout.

With bumblebees buzzing, a loud serenade,
Each flower is hopping, not one feels afraid.
The daisies complain, 'Is it time for a nap?'
While violets plot mischief, with laughter a tap.

So come heed the whispers, a floral delight,
In this fragrant kingdom, everything's bright.
With petals that prance and flora that beams,
Together we'll tumble in fluttering dreams.

Cactus Serenade

Prickly performers in desert attire,
Swaying to rhythms that never tire.
With cactus guitars, they strum with such glee,
Each note is a giggle, 'Just listen to me!'

The moon starts to chuckle, joining the band,
While sand dunes are clapping, aren't they quite grand?
A lizard on drums keeps the beats in a haze,
While sagebrush twirls in a funny maze.

With the sun behind curtains, the stars start to blink,
The coyotes join in, they're winking, I think.
The owls hoot along, "What a merry parade!"
All critters unite for a midnight charade.

So here's to the night, where laughter takes flight,
In the quirky land, everything feels right.
With prickle and cheer, the night's full of cheer,
In this cactus concert, we'll dance without fear.

Illusions of Color in the Dunes

A cactus wearing polka dots,
Waves hello with all its spots.
Sand dunes dance in wavy lines,
While lizards play on tiny shrines.

The sun throws paint across the sky,
As tumbleweeds begin to fly.
A mirage laughs with a wink,
Pulls my leg and makes me think.

Chameleons play hide-and-seek,
They're good at tricks, quite unique.
Each ripple hides a colorful tale,
Made from sand and a cool, wild gale.

Oh look, a flower wearing shades!
Hot winds blow away the jades.
They hum a tune, oh what a sight,
While singing cacti dance in light.

The Desert's Silent Symphony

Underneath the blazing sun,
Sand plays music, oh what fun!
Cacti sway with arms out wide,
While lizards giggle then they hide.

The silence sings, it's kinda weird,
Like a cactus 'n' a chameleon, cheered.
In this orchestra of rust and stone,
The squeaking shoes, you're not alone.

Balloons float high on giddy gulps,
As prickly pears tumble, oh what hulps!
Pompoms made of morning glow,
Colorful squeals, quite the show.

The sun's bright grin, it's quite a treat,
With dancing grains beneath my feet.
In the stillness, humor thrives,
A sandy joy that's full of jives.

Petals on a Windy Canvas

A cactus wears a flower hat,
Waving breezy, oh imagine that!
Colors whirl in gusty fun,
As butterflies begin to run.

Each petal flips, a beauty's jest,
Nature's nonsense, surely blessed.
In the swirl of sandy skies,
Prickly jokes and sunny sighs.

A bumblebee in a tutu spins,
Buzzing tales where chaos begins.
On grains of sand, the laughter flows,
As nature leans for a warm prose.

Through the sunlit air it gleams,
Here blooms life, or so it seems.
On this canvas of vibrant hues,
The jests of nature amuse and amuse.

Colors Bursting from Gritty Ground

From the grit, colors burst alive,
While playful lizards dive and strive.
The cacti giggle, quite a sight,
In this land of sunny delight.

The flowers shout, "Look at us bloom!"
As tumbleweeds begin to zoom.
Even rocks have silly laughs,
Making friends with dancing chaffs.

Sunflowers grow with freckled charm,
With sunflower seeds that cause alarm.
Every step, a giggle played,
In this colorful charade displayed.

Oh, sandy whims under the rays,
This boisterous land, where laughter stays.
In a canvas of colors bright,
Nature's jokes shine day and night.

The Heartbeat of a Forgotten Oasis

In a dry land where lizards play,
A cactus twirls in a quirky way.
It dreams of pools, oh what a sight,
Splashing around, it's quite a fright.

A palm tree danced, but lost its grip,
And now it's leaning on a sipping sip.
The sand critters laugh, it's quite a show,
As they sip on sunshine, don't you know?

An old well chuckles with ancient glee,
Gushing up water, not for a fee.
It whispers tales of forgotten glee,
Where flowers bloom for all to see.

So join the fun, don't be shy,
In this mirage where dreams fly high.
Let laughter echo, a joyful tune,
Under the silly smiling moon.

Silk and Sand: A Tactile Dream

A grain of sand wore a silky coat,
It fancied itself a little boat.
It floated by on a breeze so light,
Sailing through day, and drifting at night.

A tumbleweed's dance was quite the scene,
Twisting and twirling, oh so serene.
It tripped on a cactus, let out a cheer,
"Oops! Sorry folks, didn't mean to steer!"

A bed of flowers in wildly bright hues,
Giggled at bees in their vibrant shoes.
Each petal whispered, "Don't take it slow;
Join in the fun, let your worries go!"

With each gust of wind, the laughter spins,
In a land where silliness truly begins.
So dive in the mirth, let joy reclaim,
In a world where the weird is the name of the game.

A Canvas Painted by the Solar Wind

The sun paints smiles on the golden sand,
With splashes of color, it takes a stand.
A funny archer aims high with glee,
Shooting sunbeams, come play with me!

A cloud pops by in a fluffy disguise,
Winks at the sun with sparkling eyes.
Together they giggle at shadows that dance,
Creating a world where no one's a prance.

An artist sculpts with a mirage brush,
Creating giggles in a playful hush.
With every stroke, joy takes a leap,
In a landscape where silliness runs deep.

So paint your dreams with shades so bright,
In this whimsical land where laughs take flight.
Every ray carries the heart's sweet tune,
Under the watchful eye of a jolly moon.

Where the Cacti Meet the Celestial

In a field where cacti wear starry hats,
They gossip with owls and flirt with bats.
Each prickly friend has a tale to tell,
Of dancing at night while the crickets yell.

The moonbeam glances, it can't resist,
Joining the fun with a lunar twist.
"Let's have a party!" it shouts with glee,
While the night blooms with joy, wild and free.

Stars wink down, twinkling and bright,
Challenging cacti to dance through the night.
With each silly move, the cosmos sways,
In laughter-filled rhythms, the universe plays.

So come indulge in this cosmic spree,
Where sharp meets soft in perfect harmony.
In the embrace of a playful night sky,
Let the giggles and dreams soar high.

Whispers of Warmth in Aride

Cacti wear hats, oh what a sight,
Dancing in sunshine, free and bright.
Lizards in shades sip on cool drinks,
Sipping their cocktails while the sun winks.

Sand dunes giggle, rolling in mirth,
Playing hide and seek since the day of birth.
A tumbleweed waltzes, quite the show,
Who knew dry lands could put on such flow?

Petals pop out like jokes in the air,
Each bloom a stand-up with flair to spare.
The sun greets the moon with a wink and a grin,
Joking together, let the fun begin!

In this dry patch, where humor thrives,
The flora and fauna have bustling lives.
With laughter like breezes that miraculously flow,
In warm arid places, life puts on a show!

Sorrow and Splendor on Sandy Waves

Waves of warmth rise, like mirage dreams,
Seagulls tell tales of their funny schemes.
A lizard on surfboard, rides with style,
While cacti cheer on, with a gawky smile.

Oh, sandy patches do hum a tune,
Sunburnt chaps croon to the silver moon.
Pitching tents that turn into slides,
An inflatable cactus takes everyone for rides!

Shells and stones join in, making a beat,
A sandy conga line kicks up our feet.
With laughter that echoes through thin air,
Life here is wild, without a care.

Yet when the sun sets, come whispers of joy,
As light turns to shadows, no need to be coy.
For sorrow finds solace in giggles galore,
On shores that delight, who could ask for more?

The Art of Persistence in Parched Lands

A tiny sprout pokes through the dry crust,
'You think I'm done? Oh no, that's a bust!'
With grit and with laughter, it stretches and grows,
In a land where the winds make goofy old blows.

Roots dig deep down, like a joke just waiting,
For rain clouds to chuckle, no hesitating.
A cactus gets tickled by a passing breeze,
Shaking off laughter with a wobbly tease.

The sun flips a coin, comes up with a grin,
Cacti chuckle, 'Let the games begin!'
In parched solitude, where humor is found,
Persistence wears a crown, it laughs all around.

Nature's a prankster, full of surprise,
Even in thirst, life finds ways to arise.
Bouncing with joy, in this paltry scene,
What a riot it is, in lands evergreen!

Hidden Colors in a Vast Expanse

In a land of brown, blooms shine like stars,
Whispers of colors racing by in cars.
A poppy sings loudly, 'I'm here to amuse!'
While petunias giggle, slipping off their shoes.

Eagles scout high for the humor below,
Finding the funniest cacti to show.
They chuckle and dive, playing tag with the sun,
While sands play along, this game has just begun!

With laughter like rain in the heat of the day,
These hues have their fun, in a curious way.
A secret parade of colors so bright,
Showcasing their charm, in joyous delight.

In this vast expanse, where silence can bide,
Even the colors find ways to collide.
So come take a peek, listen close to the scene,
Where humor and hues dance, forever serene!

Resplendent Hues in a Gritty Paradise

In sandy pants, I found a rose,
A cactus wearing fancy clothes.
It waved at me with all its might,
In the sunlight, a silly sight.

The lizards danced, they stole the show,
With tiny moves, and even a toe!
I laughed as they flipped, oh what a thrill,
While sipping tea, I felt the chill.

A tumbleweed rolled by, oh so fast,
Chasing my hat, it had a blast.
I stood there grinning in delight,
As nature played its comical flight.

And in this land, where laughter grows,
Even the sun wears silly clothes.
So join the fun, let spirits soar,
In this gritty paradise, there's always more!

The Mirage of Serenity's Touch

I stumbled on a pool so bright,
Thought I'd dive with all my might.
But splash! It vanished with a wink,
Turns out it was just my drink!

In the quiet, whispers fun,
The rattlesnakes invite to run.
They slithered by with a silly grin,
Saying, 'Do you really want to swim?'

The sun was hot, I lost my hat,
It flew away—how rude is that?
It waved goodbye, my golden crown,
While I just flopped and flopped around.

A wise old cactus, full of glee,
Said, 'Join the laughter, drink some tea!'
So we toasted to mirth 'neath skies of blue,
In the mirage where joy sticks like glue.

Awakening Beauty in Dry Lands

In a land where flowers rarely speak,
A bloom appeared, oh what a freak!
It sang a song with a squeaky voice,
Made me giggle, oh what a choice!

A tumble of colors, bright and bold,
Adventures waiting to be told.
The cacti giggled, 'What's the fuss?'
'We're just here making a ruckus!'

I found a lizard with shades so fine,
He danced on rocks, claiming they shine.
With a flick of his tail, he took a bow,
I couldn't help but laugh, oh wow!

So beneath the sun, with skies so wide,
Laughter echoed, joy won't hide.
In dry lands where magic thrives,
Awakening beauty keeps us alive!

Dancing Shadows on Cracked Surfaces

A shadow danced across the ground,
In wobbly moves, it twirled around.
'Hey, get down!' I screamed with glee,
'But not too much or you'll scare me!'

The sun painted shapes like silly clowns,
As giggles echoed through the towns.
With every step, the rocks did quake,
And all the critters joined in to shake.

A mirage hovered, played peek-a-boo,
I chased it down; how about you?
It laughed and hid, then would return,
In this game of joy for which we yearn.

So if you see those shadows prance,
Join the fun, take a chance.
In the cracks where laughter grows,
Dancing shadows are how it goes!

Sands of Color

A cactus dons a vibrant hat,
While lizards sip on tea and chat.
The tumbleweeds join in the spree,
Dancing to a tune from the cacti tree.

Scarabs wear shoes of shiny foil,
As sunflowers plot with soil to spoil.
The while winds swirl with giggles loud,
As nature's jesters gather round.

Ants in tuxedos parade so fine,
Throwing confetti from their divine.
The sand shimmers with laughter bright,
In this wild party under the sunlight.

Jokes bounce around like bouncing balls,
With wise old owls sharing their calls.
In this playful land of vibrant flair,
Even the sun seems to stop and stare.

Mirage of Petals

The flowers wink in the hot, dry air,
As bees play tricks without a care.
A mirage giggles, 'Come take a look,'
But it just vanishes like a worn-out book.

Mice in sneakers dash with speed,
Competing for crumbs, oh, what a breed!
The petals blush when the wind sings,
A symphony of laughter on bright wings.

Cacti with sunglasses serve lemonade,
While shadows joke in the cool glade.
"Why did the sprout cross the sand?" they tease,
"To find something fun, if you please!"

In a land where humor grows like weeds,
The flowers share their giggling creeds.
Beneath the sun's never-ending dome,
Even the earth feels a bit more like home.

Oasis Whispers

In the heart of the sun, a pool of tricks,
Where frogs wear tiny boots and flicks.
The palm trees rub their leafy hands,
While squirrels tell tales of far-off lands.

Ducks quack puns with a splashy flair,
While frogs croon ballads into the air.
The oasis chuckles in sugar and spice,
As the lizards perform a playful dice.

A turtle in shades naps on the shore,
Dreaming of races and secret lore.
"Run like the wind," the breeze seems to boast,
But the turtle just smiles, the chill, he'll toast.

The water sparkles with stories untold,
As laughter glimmers like liquid gold.
In this sanctuary, all life's a jest,
Where even the sun takes a playful rest.

Life in Arid Embrace

In a wild land where the odd might thrive,
Chameleons wear shades yet still connive.
The sun sets low, the shadows play,
In the heat's embrace, they dance all day.

Beetles in bowties pull pranks on friends,
While the sagebrush plots how fun never ends.
Rabbits flip coins, a game of chance,
While the moon starts to waltz in a silvery dance.

Silly squirrels with acrobatic flair,
Leap over cacti without a care.
"Why don't we travel," they giggle and scheme,
"To places unseen, in a wild, mad dream?"

From the dunes to the stars, the laughter rolls,
In this quirky land, creativity strolls.
With each grain of sand, a chuckle to share,
In life's arid embrace, fun's everywhere!

The Color of Resilience

In the sand, a cactus stands proud,
Wearing a party hat, looking so loud.
It dances in sun, a wobbly groove,
Who knew prickly could also be smooth?

A lizard sips tea, pinky in air,
Sipping with critters, without a care.
Each cacti comic holds laughter tight,
Spinning tales 'neath the twinkling light.

A mirage passes by, a wild parade,
With lollipops and confetti, it's made.
Smiles overlapping like blooms in a rush,
Each chuckle ignites an oasis of hush.

A tumbleweed rolls, he thinks he's a star,
Dancing alone, he's gone too far.
But in this expanse, joy takes its chance,
Finding life's humor in each silly dance.

Visions in the Valley

A wind-swept face on a rock, so wise,
Winks at the tumbleweeds that twist and rise.
Each blade of grass sings a tune, offbeat,
In this valley where the quirky folk meet.

A cholla in shades, a hat from the sun,
Claims he's a cactus who's just out for fun.
Cactuses gossip, their spines all a-flick,
About little creatures who make magic stick.

A squirrel on stilts, what a sight to behold!
He recites funny poems, brave and bold.
These visions invite much laughter and cheer,
In the valley where laughter's all we hear.

Cactus kids giggle, growing up quick,
With dreams and pranks, they're full of the trick.
And under the sun, they bounce and they beam,
Creating a riot, life's whimsical dream!

Ripples of Vitality

In the heat, water's a mischievous jester,
Making puddles dance, oh what a tester.
A mirage slips in, with a wink and a slide,
It tickles the ground, then runs off to hide.

A rabbit hops by, wearing big clown shoes,
Juggling bright berries, singing the blues.
The rocks laugh along, as they tumble and roll,
In a rhythm of joy, that brightens the soul.

Each ripple in air, sends giggles galore,
As shadows skip past, then dance on the floor.
The air smells of humor, sweet and refined,
As silly life jokes are shared, intertwined.

A flock of bold birds takes flight in a line,
Mimicking jumps, oh aren't they divine?
With laughter like ripples that spark in the day,
Vitality blooms in this wild, funny way.

Wilderness of Flourishing Dreams

In the wild, a band of flowers unite,
Practicing stand-up, oh what a sight!
They tickle the air with their jokes and glee,
As bees buzz around, taking notes on the spree.

A sunflower winks at the moon while it's out,
Saying, "Don't trip, it's a long way about!"
The daisies all snicker, their petals aglow,
In this wilderness, humor runs the show.

Little critters in coats of bright plaid,
Tell tales of mischief, life's wacky and mad.
With each silly story, their roots grow in cheer,
Flourishing dreams as they laugh without fear.

So here in the wild, life's funny refrain,
Reminds us to smile through joy and through pain.
Under the sun, intertwined, we'll chase,
The wilderness thrives, a whimsical space.

Petals Against the Wind of Time

A cactus danced in a foolish spree,
With blooms that waved like a wobbly bee.
The sun wore shades, looking quite surreal,
While prickly friends spun around with zeal.

With laughter echoing across the sand,
Giggling blooms took a colorful stand.
A tumbleweed twirled in a happy chase,
As flowers rapped in a comical race.

Cacti tried their best to throw a party,
In their spiny suits, looking quite hearty.
The wind played tunes that made them sway,
Petals performed in a fanciful ballet.

Their colors splashed like confetti bright,
In a goofy showdown, they all took flight.
While shadows giggled beneath the light,
Time tickled petals, a whimsical sight.

The Symphony of Sparse Existence

In a land where not much grows, you see,
A tiny bloom struts with glee.
It wears a sombrero made of rays,
Singing to cacti in funny ways.

A lilting tune on the wind did play,
As tumbleweeds joined the charade ballet.
Sparse existence? More like a jam,
Where flowers sneeze and bumblebees slam.

They held hands with the dry, dusty air,
In a duet of laughter, without a care.
Each petal wobbled, off beat but spry,
While sunburnt ants sang their own lullaby.

So here in the dust, a concert unfolds,
With silly notes in bright greens and golds.
Not a lot of room, but who needs a crowd?
In this quirky theater, they all sang loud.

Surreal Colors Amidst the Grit

Amidst the grit, a wild colors' show,
With echoes of laughter where no winds blow.
Cacti in polka dots scream for attention,
While a rainbow chases shadows in detention.

Petals whispered secrets to stubborn stones,
Having debates around the brittle bones.
A sunset giggled, dipped in a jar,
As flowers went camping beneath a star.

Laughter painted the horizon bright,
While dry leaves played tag till the fall of night.
Napping with humor, the moon chimed in,
As petals and shadows participated in sin.

A surreal circus in arid delight,
Where colors threw parties, oh what a sight!
With chuckles and grins, they broke through the grit,
A joyous parade, not a bloom to omit.

Threads of Life in the Midst of Silence

In a quiet sprawl, a curious tale,
Of threads spinning laughter, tiny and frail.
A worm in a top hat, oh what a sight,
Swayed with the daisies, all dressed up tight.

A tumbleweed wobbled, unsure and bold,
While dusty bugs juggled leaves big and old.
In silence, they found the wildest of fun,
As the moon cracked jokes, one by one.

Every petal told stories without a word,
Painting the air with the laughter unheard.
With roots deep in whimsy, they spun and swirled,
While stories of life in silence unfurled.

Threads wove together in mischief and cheer,
As shadows danced lightly, drawing near.
In the hush of the sands, here blooms a delight,
A riddle of life, held tight in the night.

www.ingramcontent.com/pod-product-compliance
Lightning Source LLC
Chambersburg PA
CBHW071814160426
43209CB00003B/84